RECEIVE YE
THE HOLY GHOST

RECEIVE YE THE HOLY GHOST

By

A.A. Allen

Printed in the United States of America and Australia.

Bottom of the Hill Publishing

Memphis, TN

www.BottomoftheHillPublishing.com

ISBN: 978-1-61203-493-5

Content

A. A. Allen

CHAPTER 1

THE PROMISE OF THE HOLY GHOST

The last sermon preached by Christ before His ascension was on the Holy Ghost! He said, "... wait for the promise of the Father ... ye shall be baptized with the Holy Ghost not many days hence." Acts 1:4-5. (See also Acts 1:8-9) Luke records the last words of Christ as, "Behold I send the promise of my Father upon you; but tarry ye in the city of Jerusalem until ye be endued with power from on high." Luke 24:49. This message must have been of utmost importance, or Christ would never have reserved it until just before He ascended.

John the Baptist promised, "He shall baptize YOU with the Holy Ghost and with fire." Matt. 3:11.

Eight hundred years before Calvary, the prophet Joel prophesied, 'I will pour out my spirit upon ALL flesh and your sons and daughters shall . . ." Joel 2:28. This promise was fulfilled in the second chapter of Acts, for Peter, one of the one hundred and twenty that was filled on that day said, "This is that which was spoken by the prophet Joel." Acts 2:16-18. Later, Peter speaking to a multitude (Acts 2:6) said, "The promise is unto you and to your children, and to all that are afar off , even as many as the Lord our God shall call." Acts 2:38-39.

Can God's promise fail? No! A million times no! "For ALL the promises of God in him are yea and in him Amen." II Cor. 1:20.

CHAPTER 2

TO WHOM HAS GOD PROMISED THE HOLY GHOST?

This experience is promised to saved people of every age. In Peter's preaching, the list included YOU, YOUR CHILDREN, THOSE AFAR OFF, and even as many as the Lord our God shall call. He also includes all those who have repented. Acts 2:39. It matters not who YOU or YOUR CHILDREN are, or how "afar off" you or they may be, all are on the list.

John, preaching to a "multitude" (Luke 3:7), said, "He shall baptize YOU with the Holy Ghost." V. 16. Then the promise is for any or all the multitude who will meet the condition, for all God's promises are conditional.

Joel said it was for ALL flesh. Joel 2:28. However, that "flesh" must be obedient according to Acts 5:32, "... so is also the Holy Ghost, whom God hath given to them that OBEY him."

Certainly everyone needs this experience today. Even Mary the mother of Jesus, whom the Lord chose, because of her purity, to be the mother of Jesus, felt her need for appropriating this promise. She was among the first to receive. Acts 1:14.

Jesus said, "Ye shall receive power after that the Holy Ghost is come upon you." Acts 1:8. This is God's recipe for POWER. Every Christian needs it, should desire and earnestly seek it.

This experience is not a mere privilege but rather a direct command. "'And being assembled together with them, COMMANDED THEM that they should not depart from Jerusalem but wait for the promise of the Father." Acts 1:4. So, YOU ARE COMMANDED to be filled! Do you love the Lord? You say, "Of course I love Jesus." Then, there is one way you can prove that you love him and that is by keeping his commandments, and one of his commandments is that YOU BE FILLED. Jesus said, "If you love me KEEP my commandments." Then if you really love the Lord, you will do as he has commanded, and . . . "BE FILLED WITH THE SPIRIT." Eph. 5:18.

So there is scriptural evidence that YOU need to be filled with the Holy Spirit because you need POWER.

You can have no excuse for not having received this experience inasmuch as it has been promised to YOU!

Further, since you have been COMMANDED to be filled, there is but one thing for you to do. Settle this here and now that you are going to have this experience NOW!

CHAPTER 3

IS CONVERSION THE SAME AS THE BAPTISM OF THE HOLY GHOST?

Regeneration ' conversion ' confession ' confirmation New Birth or whatever you may call being saved, is not the Baptism in the Holy Spirit. Salvation is the first step, and of course very wonderful, but the Baptism in the Holy Spirit is a different experience. Those who believe that the Baptism in the Holy Spirit is identical with the New Birth base their belief upon I Corinthians 12:13, "For by one Spirit are we all baptized into one body, . . . and have been made to drink into one Spirit." They say this verse teaches that when the sinner repents he receives the Baptism in the Holy Spirit, and thus enters into the spiritual body of Christ: but this verse rather shows that it is the Holy Spirit who brings each member into the body of Christ by an immersion into it. Thus the baptism in the Holy

Spirit and the baptism into the body of Christ are not synonymous terms.

No, these are two separate and distinct experiences. Peter said, "Repent and be baptized (now) . . . and ye shall (future) receive the gift of the Holy Ghost." Acts 2:38. Here it is plain that salvation is a different experience than the Baptism with the Holy Ghost.

It is possible for one to be saved and filled with the Holy Spirit almost simultaneously or one may receive this experience the same day or night, but he receives two separate and distinct experiences. That one does not receive both experiences in one is shown by the fact that the disciples were saved men, had their "names written in heaven." Luke 10:20 (See also John 17:6; John 13:10.) However, they were told by Christ to "wait for the promise of the Father." Acts 1:4-5. It was still in the future. "And behold, I send the promise of the Father upon you: but tarry ye in the city of Jerusalem, until ye be endued with power from on high." Luke 24:49.

The Samaritans were converted, had "given heed" to the word of God, and many had received healing. They had also been baptized in water. Acts 8:5-12. They did not receive the Holy Ghost until later (v. 16) when Peter and John laid their hands upon them. Acts 8:17.

The Apostle Paul was converted on the road to Damascus. Acts 9:1-6. He did not receive the Holy Ghost until three days later. verse 17.

The twelve men at Ephesus were saved men, called "disciples." They were asked, "Have ye received the Holy Ghost SINCE (not when) ye believed?" Acts 19:2. They were baptized in water in the fifth verse, but did not receive the Holy Ghost until Paul laid hands upon them in the sixth verse.

At conversion the Christian is

not filled with the Holy Spirit (Holy Ghost and Holy Spirit used inter-changeably), but made simply a partaker of the "Spirit of Christ." "If any man have not the SPIRIT OF CHRIST, he is none of his." Rom. 8:9. This spirit received at conversion is the spirit of Christ the second person of the Trinity, not the Holy Spirit, who is the THIRD person of the Godhead. Just as every person created in God's image has a spirit, even so God Himself (the Father, the FIRST person of the trinity) has a spirit. His

Son (Christ, the SECOND person of the trinity), being the express image of His Father, also has a spirit which is distinctly His own 'the "Spirit of Christ." (Luke 23:46) Both these spirits are distinct from, yet in complete harmony with, THE HOLY SPIRIT, who is a distinct personality' not merely the spirit of another and is the THIRD person of the trinity. (Spoken of as HE, never "it").

It is the "Spirit of Christ" (Rom. 8:9. 16) that "beareth witness with our spirit that we are the children of God." It was to His OWN children (and "if any man have not the Spirit of Christ he in none of His") that Jesus was speaking when He said, "I will pray the Father, and He shall give you another Comforter, that he may abide with you forever; even the Spirit of truth; WHOM the world cannot receive, because it seeth HIM not, neither knoweth HIM: but ye know HIM; for HE dwelleth with you, AND SHALL BE IN YOU." John 14:16-17.

One must remember there is a vast difference between having the abiding presence of the Spirit WITH YOU and being baptized or literally FILLED WITH the Holy Ghost.

WATER BAPTISM IS NOT THE BAPTISM IN THE HOLY SPIRIT. However, it is a Biblical teaching, and I believe all should be baptized in water according to the formula Jesus gave (Matthew 28:19). In Philip's revival at Samaria some had been baptized in water, but not until Peter and John came did they receive the Baptism in the Holy

Spirit (Acts 8). Simon had been baptized in water (Acts 8:13), but he had not received the Baptism in the Holy Spirit.

Cornelius and his company received the Baptism in the Holy Spirit but were baptized in water after receiving that experience (Acts 10:46, 47).

Someone has said that Paul baptized the Ephesian Christians in water and they received the Holy Spirit (Acts 19:1-7). Paul re-baptized them as they had only John's baptism unto repentance, which, seemingly, was quite different to our baptism in water, typical of the death, burial, and resurrection of the Lord Jesus Christ. But it was AFTER Paul had baptized them, that he laid his hands upon them, and the Holy Spirit came upon them (verse 6). It may have been an hour afterward or a day, at least it was afterward.

Water baptism may, or may not be, administered before receiving the Baptism in the Holy Spirit, but water baptism, definitely, is not the

Baptism in the Holy Spirit.

SANCTIFICATION IS NOT THE BAPTISM IN THE HOLY SPIRIT. Sanctification is very blessed and definite. It means to free or set apart from sin. When we are saved the blood of Jesus washes us free from sin, or sets us apart from our past sins. Because of the washing of the blood each sin is placed into the sea of His forgetfulness. Hallelujah! This phase of sanctification, then, is instantaneous, taking place at conversion (Hebrew 13:12.) This does not necessarily mean that one cannot sin again. Paul wrote to the church at Corinth and addressed them as "saints" or literally "sanctified ones" (I Corinthians 1:2; 6:11); yet many of them were very carnal, some even living in open sin (I Corinthians 3:1; 5:1, 2, 7, 8).

We can readily see, then, that not only does sanctification have an instantaneous phase, but it is also a progressive work. With the apostle Paul in Phillippians 3:12-14, we "press toward the mark." We are changed into the image of the Lord from glory to glory (II Corinthians 3:18).

Old man "self" is to be crucified. Sometimes this is not as quick a process as many feel it is, but we must "press toward the mark," for, we "should not serve sin." When we see Him, we shall be like Him (I John 3:2). Yes, sanctification is a definite, glorious Biblical teaching, but it is not the 'Baptism in the Holy Spirit.

CHAPTER 4

DO ALL SPEAK WITH TONGUES?

Many today say, "I think you can receive the Holy Ghost without speaking with tongues. After all, there are nine gifts of the Spirit mentioned in I Cor. 12. Why should not some other gift do just as well, as evidence that one has received the baptism with the Spirit?"

First of all, because God has never used any other gift in that way, as far as the scripture record is concerned.

On the day of Pentecost, when the Holy Ghost was first given, about a hundred and twenty people, including the apostles, "the women," Mary the mother of Jesus, and his brethren (Acts 1:13-15), were gathered together in one accord (Acts

2:1), in an upper room where they had "all continued with one accord in prayer and supplication" (Acts 1:14), when suddenly "They were all filled with the Holy Ghost, and began to speak with other tongues, as the Spirit gave them utterance." Acts 2:4.

About eight years later, Peter preached the gospel for the first time to Gentiles, a group of friends and kinsmen of Cornelius, a Roman Centurion. These all believed the preaching of Peter, "that through his name whosoever believeth in him shall receive remission of sins." Acts 10:43. God, purifying their hearts by faith (Acts 15:9), baptized all them which heard the word, while Peter was yet speaking. (Acts 10:44.) Six Jewish believers who had come with Peter from Joppa heard them speak with tongues, and although they were surprised that Gentiles could receive the Holy Ghost, they were immediately fully persuaded that THAT VERY THING had taken place! "For they heard them speak with tongues and magnify God." Acts 10:46. They did not know the Gentiles had received the Holy Ghost because they had been baptized in water, for this did not happen until later (see v. 47-48). They did not know it because Peter had laid hands on them, for he had not done this. They did not claim to recognize the fact through a direct revelation from heaven. They declared that they knew it "FOR (because) they heard them speak with tongues!" (v. 46). While there were many gathered together upon whom the Spirit fell on this occasion, NO OTHER GIFT is mentioned as evidence that they had received Him. THEY SPOKE WITH TONGUES! That was enough to convince Peter, his six friends from Joppa, and even the apostles at Jerusalem. Acts 11:15, 17. This evidence so thoroughly convinced Peter that in his defense to the apostles and brethren at Jerusalem, who contended with him and rebuked him for going to the Gentiles, when he had told them the story, he concluded his defense with the words, "Forasmuch then as God gave them THE LIKE GIFT as he did unto us, who believed on the Lord Jesus Christ; what was I that I could WITHSTAND GOD?" Acts 11:17.

Many professed religious leaders today seem to be much more courageous than Peter, for they do not hesitate to withstand God in this matter!

Many profess themselves to be willing to allow the Spirit to dwell in them, IF HE JUST WOULDN'T ASK TO HAVE CONTROL OF THEIR TONGUE! This is not strange, since God has told us plainly that "the tongue can no man tame; it is an unruly evil." James 3:8. This, then, may readily be expected to be the last member of the body to submit to the Spirit. Yet no man can be FULLY yielded to the Spirit, completely submerged (immersed, baptized) in the Spirit, until the tongue is yielded too!

Would you accept an invitation to dwell in a friend's house, if he should say "Just move right in and make yourself at home. The whole house is at your disposal. You may use any part of it as though it were your own. All I ask is that you do not speak. Just don't speak, and you are entirely welcome." I dare say, you would look for other quarters!

Include the right to speak in your invitation to the Holy Spirit to make your body His Temple, and (if you also can offer Him a clean dwelling), He will be happy to accept your invitation!

Friend, do not resist the Holy Ghost! Do not try to WITHSTAND GOD!

More than twenty years after the day of Pentecost, Paul in his missionary travels came to Ephesus, and there found a group of believers who had not so much as heard "whether there be any Holy Ghost." Acts 19:1-6. Yet when the Holy Ghost came upon them, the same thing happened as on the day of Pentecost. "When Paul laid his hands upon them, the Holy Ghost came on them; and THEY SPOKE WITH TONGUES, and prophesied." Acts 19:6. The pattern was still unchanged.

Here, another gift of the Spirit is mentioned, but only as appearing ALONG WITH speaking with tongues. Nowhere in the Scripture is ANY OTHER GIFT mentioned

ALONE in connection with the receiving of the Holy Ghost. One hundred and twenty on the day of Pentecost, twelve at Ephesus, and "many" at the house of Cornelius ALL spoke with tongues. Does it not seem strange that if some other gift would do just as well, that some out of this great number did not receive some other gift instead of tongues as evidence?

A young man may give his bride-to-be many GIFTS, but only one the engagement ring is taken to be evidence that she is his chosen bride. The Spirit gives many gifts, but ONLY speaking with other tongues is accepted as evidence of having been filled with the Spirit. What maiden would accept her lover, receive his other gifts, and yet be ashamed to wear his ring before her friends? If she truly loves and honors him, she will wear it proudly!

Speaking in tongues as the initial physical evidence that one has received the Holy Ghost is the same in essence and origin as the gift of tongues listed in I Cor. 12 along with eight others, which the Spirit divided among Spirit-filled believers "to every man severally as he will." But it is different in purpose and use. It is also different in that the phenomena of Pentecost was clearly declared to be available to "all flesh" (Acts 2:17), while the GIFT OF TONGUES is to be bestowed "as He will" (I Cor. 12:11), and is for use in the public assembly.

Many today argue that Paul said, "Do all speak with tongues?", inferring that the expected answer is "No." Note that this chapter, I Cor. 12, does not deal with receiving the baptism of the Holy Ghost. It is written for the express purpose of dispelling ignorance in regard to SPIRITUAL GIFTS, of which speaking in tongues is one. It deals with spiritual GIFTS (plural) and does not discuss the GIFT (singular) of the Holy Ghost. This Gift is discussed, exemplified, and illustrated in the book of Acts, where in every case that mentions any identifying mark, that mark is SPEAKING WITH TONGUES. The GIFT of the Holy Ghost is an experience which comes as a baptism, ONCE to the believer. AFTERWARD, God has planned to give other GIFTS, listed in I Cor. 12:8-10. Their use is divided among various members of the group, and is for the benefit of the entire group, "to profit withal." I Cor. 12:7. None of these gifts have ceased, but ALL are available to God's people today, "For the perfecting of the saints, for the work of the ministry, for the edifying of the body of Christ: TILL WE ALL COME IN THE UNITY OF THE FAITH, AND OF THE KNOWLEDGE OF THE SON OF GOD, UNTO THE MEASURE OF THE STATURE OF THE FULLNESS OF CHRIST." Eph. 4:12, 13. Yet it is plain that these gifts as exercised in this life are "in part," imperfect and incomplete, and shall eventually be done away. I Cor. 13:8, 9, 10. Yet, let us not be deceived as to the time when this shall take place. "WHEN THAT WHICH IS PERFECT

IS COME, THEN THAT WHICH IS IN PART SHALL BE DONE AWAY." Verse 10. "For now we see through a glass darkly; but then FACE TO FACE." Verse 12. This is in perfect agreement with Eph. 4:12, 13. Certainly the saints are NOT yet perfected, are NOT in unity of the faith, do NOT know the Son of God fully, nor have they attained to perfection, nor to the measure of the stature of the fullness of

Christ. When we see Him face to face then we shall be perfect, like Him (I John 3:2), and shall no longer need these gifts which are in part, for we shall know all things. Paul's purpose in writing I Cor. 12, 13 and 14, was to give instructions in the proper use of these gifts in the churches from the time that they were written until the end of the age, when Jesus should come to take His church away.

We are instructed in regard to the gift of tongues that it should be by two, or at the most by three, and that by course (one at a time), and that it should be interpreted, or else that he should keep silence in the church. (I Cor. 14:27.)

Yet on the day of Pentecost, one hundred and twenty ALL began to speak with tongues. At Ephesus, twelve spoke with tongues, and at the house of Cornelius "all that heard the word" began to speak with tongues, right during the sermon. And there is no record that any of it was interpreted. Paul said, "I would that YE ALL spoke with tongues." I Cor 14:5. For 'He that speaketh in an unknown tongue edifieth himself' (verse 4), and "speaketh . . .unto God" (verse 2).

Paul never intended that the instructions given in I Cor. 14 should be taken for a condemnation of speaking with tongues, for he tells us in the same chapter, "I would that ye ALL spoke with tongues (I Cor. 14:5), and "Forbid NOT to speak with tongues" (verse 39).

Speaking with tongues is peculiarly suited for use as evidence of this new experience, which according to Joel 2:28 had been reserved for "afterward," which Peter interprets as "the last days." Acts 2:17. Never before had the Holy Ghost been given as Joel had prophesied, for Peter, speaking by the Spirit of God, declares clearly that "this is that." Jesus Himself made it plain that the Holy Ghost was not to be given until after His ascension. "But this spoke he of the Spirit, which they that believe should receive:

FOR THE HOLY GHOST WAS NOT YET GIVEN: BECAUSE THAT JESUS WAS NOT YET GLORIFIED." John 6:39.

If prophecy could be taken as evidence of the Baptism of the Spirit, then all the Old Testament prophets from Enoch to Malachi were baptized with the Spirit, for these "holy men of God spoke as they were moved by the Holy Ghost." II Pet. 1:21. But these were not baptized with the Holy Ghost, for the Holy Spirit was not yet given. They were only "MOVED" by the Holy Ghost.

The gifts of healing and miracles could not serve as evidence of this new fullness of the Spirit, for Elijah and Elisha both healed the sick, raised the dead, and worked miracles. Yet they had not received the baptism of the Holy Ghost, for it had not yet been given!

Daniel was given wisdom (Dan. 2:14), knowledge (Dan. 2:28), interpretation (Dan. 5:26), and faith (Heb. 11:33). Yet he lived many years before the "last day" outpouring of the Spirit.

Elisha discerned the greedy spirit of Gehazi, when he followed Naaman to take for himself by craft those things which he coveted. (See II Kings 5:26.)

Before the day of Pentecost, NO ONE EVER SPOKE IN AN UNLEARNED TONGUE, as he was moved by the Holy Ghost, or "as the Spirit gave utterance." On the day of Pentecost, "They were all FILLED WITH THE HOLY GHOST, and BEGAN to speak with tongues, as the Spirit gave them utterance." Acts 2:4. They BEGAN at Pentecost, and, praise God, they haven't stopped yet! Even to this day, those who are filled with the Holy Ghost give evidence of having been filled by

SPEAKING WITH TONGUES! Of no other gift could it be truthfully said that they BEGAN on the day of Pentecost. This latter day outpouring of the Spirit was a new experience for a new dispensation, marked by a new manifestation of the Spirit, SPEAKING WITH TONGUES. This new manifestation was recognized by believers in the early church as being the uniform and undisputed evidence of the presence of the experience. (Note Acts 10:46, 11:15-17.)

God spoke throughout His dispensation. He spoke to Moses at the burning bush (Ex. 3 and 4) , calling him by name, and identifying Himself as "I AM" the eternal God. He spoke to Abram (Gen. 12:1), and Joshua (Josh. 1:1). He spoke to Isaiah, saying "With stammering lips and another tongue will he speak to this people, to whom he said, this is the rest wherewith ye may cause the weary to rest; and this is the refreshing." Isa. 28:11, 12). (Applied by Paul to this situation, I Cor. 14:21-22.) God SAID it would happen, and it did!

Jesus spoke throughout His stay on earth. His words were "spirit and life." John 6:63. He declared that one of the signs which should follow them that believe should be "They shall speak with new tongues." Mark 16:17. He also declared that "When the Comforter is come . . . even the Spirit of truth, which proceedeth from the Father, HE SHALL TESTIFY OF ME." John 15:26. "Whatsoever he shall hear, that shall he SPEAK." John 16:13. Jesus said he would speak, and he did!

He still speaks today. ALL FLESH may enter into God's promise, if they be willing and obedient, and receive the outpouring of the Holy Ghost as the disciples did at Pentecost, complete with the scriptural evidence of speaking with tongues.

But some will say, "The Samaritans didn't speak with tongues." How do you know they didn't? Certainly the Bible does NOT say that they didn't! It does not say that the fact was recognized by some OTHER MANIFESTATION. How, then, was it known that they received the Holy Ghost? What did Simon see that caused him to desire to be able to bestow the Holy Ghost by the laying on of his hands? Simon was a sorcerer (magician). He had been attracted to the Christians by the mighty miracles and signs which he had seen done under the ministry of Philip. He was not a spiritual man, but was impressed by the presence of outward, visible, audible signs. He was impressed with the thing which happened when Peter and John laid their hands upon these people and they received the Holy Ghost! He saw in this a "magic" which far outreached his former sorceries, and desired to add it to his stock. He did not offer money for the power to lay his hands upon people and say to them "receive ye the Holy Ghost. Take it by faith. Act just like you have always acted." He offered his money for a DISTINCTLY SUPERNATURAL GIFT! If it wasn't the power to cause people to speak with new tongues, WHAT WAS IT? If the Samaritans didn't speak with tongues WHAT DID THEY DO? All well-known Biblical authorities before 1900 declared that "They probably spoke with tongues."

Did Paul speak with tongues? Acts 9:17 does not mention tongues. Yet it is certain that at some time, Paul began to speak with tongues, for he personally declared "I thank my God I speak with tongues more than ye all." I Cor. 14:18. There is little doubt that, like the one hundred and twenty on the day of Pentecost, he BEGAN to speak with tongues WHEN HE WAS BAPTIZED WITH THE HOLY GHOST!

Why did not the inspired writer mention tongues in these cases? For the simple reason that the pattern had already been established. The very fact that tongues are not mentioned in these cases makes it even more plain that speaking with tongues was ALREADY RECOGNIZED AS THE NORMAL ACCOMPANIMENT of the Baptism with the Holy Ghost' inasmuch as no other gift is mentioned as evidence in these cases. Having given this manifestation as evidence in every case where any evidence is mentioned would make it very needful that if some other manifestation were to be accepted in some cases, there would need to be at least ONE record of such a case. There is no such record.

When you go to buy a set of tea cups, do you always say, "Be sure to include the handles'? No! You take the handles for granted. Tea cups HAVE handles! The pattern has already been established. Just so, speaking in tongues has become the established pattern in receiving the baptism with the Holy Ghost.

This pattern is very apparent in Acts 10 and 11. Although Acts 10:45, 46 declares that Peter and his Jewish friends knew the Gentiles had received the Holy Ghost because "(For) they heard them speak with tongues," yet in chapter 11, Peter does not mention tongues in his defense before the apostles, but rather points out that there could be no denying that God had given the Holy Spirit to the Gentiles also BECAUSE WHAT THEY HAD

RECEIVED WAS ACCORDING TO THE RECOGNIZED PATTERN! Acts 11:15, 17 "The Holy Ghost fell on them AS ON US AT THE BEGINNING . . . Forasmuch then as God gave them THE LIKE GIFT AS HE DID UNTO US who believed on the Lord Jesus Christ; what was I that I could withstand God?" The fact that the original and accepted manifestation of the infilling of the Spirit was present at the Gentile household was sufficient not only to convince Peter, his Jewish friends, the Apostles and the Council at Jerusalem, but even to revolutionize the entire attitude of the early church toward the Gentiles. Speaking in tongues at the house of Cornelius, and THAT ALONE, was sufficient to persuade every Jewish Christian that God had broken down the wall of partition and given Christianity in all its fullness and glory to the Gentiles, who had always been regarded as "dogs," (Mark 7:27, 28) and as 'unclean", (Acts 10:9-20.)

(Note: Peter did not say, "The like gift as He did unto us the APOS-

TLES", but "The like gift as He did unto us WHO BELIEVED", thus including any other of the Jewish fellowship who had obeyed the exortation of Acts 2:38 SINCE the day of Pentecost. This defense was not before the Apostles only, but before the "Apostles and brethren that were in Judea." Acts 11:1.)

Other manifestations may accompany speaking with tongues, such as prophecy, visions, and dreams (see Acts 2:17; 19:6). Yet these do not crowd out speaking with tongues.

If you have never spoken with tongues, how can you know that you have received the Holy Ghost? How can you prove by the scripture that you have received an experience beyond that given to Old Testament saints, and set apart for the "last days?" Acts 2:17; Joel 2:28. But you say, "I certainly got SOMETHING!" Certainly you did. So did the Old Testament saints. You say, "I know what I got was from God." There is no reason to doubt it, but WAS IT THE BAPTISM OF THE

HOLY GHOST? How do you KNOW it was? What you got was GOOD, but should it stand in your way, and keep you from pressing on, and being filled with the Holy Ghost, as God planned that His people should be in the LAST DAYS? Don't lose what God has given you, but go on from there and be filled with the Spirit, immersed, controlled, baptized with the Spirit! Soul, mind, spirit, body, hands, tongue, lips, voice, and ALL!

CHAPTER 5

INSTRUCTIONS TO THOSE SEEKING THE HOLY GHOST

Remember that faith (on your part) has a part in the baptism of the Holy Ghost. Concerning the Holy Ghost, Jesus said, "If ye then, being evil, know how to give good gifts to your children: how much more shall your heavenly Father give the Holy Spirit to them that ASK Him?" Luke 11:13.

In asking, you MUST "ask in faith, nothing wavering. For he that wavereth is like a wave of the sea driven with the wind and tossed. For LET NOT THAT MAN THINK THAT HE SHALL RECEIVE ANYTHING OF THE LORD." James 1:6-7.

There is but one way to ask in

faith. This is found in Mark 11:24. "What things so ever ye desire, when ye pray, BELIEVE THAT YE RECEIVE THEM, AND YOU SHALL HAVE THEM." The moment you BELIEVE YOU RECEIVE, God will fill you.

If you find it hard to believe that God will FILL YOU NOW, it would be wise for you to search your heart for the reason. The Bible teaches that there are definite hindrances to real faith. Eliminate the hindrances and the result will be FAITH THAT CANNOT BE DEFEATED, OR DIS-COURAGED, OR FAIL! If you have my book titled "GOD'S GUARANTEE TO HEAL YOU," read chapter six, "Have the Faith That God Gives," and chapter seven, "Hindrances to Faith." Sin, disobedience and self-will destroy or murder faith (confidence). (See I John 3:21; Isaiah 59:1; Psa. 66:18; I Peter 3:7.)

The Holy Spirit is "given to them that obey him" (Acts 5:32), and is not even promised to the "children of disobedience" (Eph. 5:6). When you can present to God a pure heart and clean hands, then you can approach God scripturally, "lifting up holy hands" (I Tim. 2:8), and praising God with a joy born of faith, knowing that the promise is for YOU!

If your faith has not yet mounted to this point, seek God earnestly, and search your heart. Do not condemn yourself and become discouraged, but wait in His presence, where the light of God's word, applied by His Spirit, can reveal to you those things which as yet need to be corrected before you can have real faith. "Enter into his gates with thanksgiving, and into his courts with praise." Psa. 100:4. Praise Him for what HE IS, for what He has ALREADY DONE, and for His faithful promise to give to YOU the power which He has promised (Acts 1:8), just as soon as you are obedient (Acts 5:32), and ready. Wait patiently in His presence, in an attitude of worship, with praise, and holy hands uplifted. You will not be waiting long. God will fill you, or show you the hindrance. If He shows you some disobedience, or some broken vow, do not think that you can buy the baptism of the Holy Ghost with words of praise, without repentance, and perhaps even restitution if it be possible. Words of praise will not buy it, any more than Simon's money. (Acts 8:20)

Ask God to fill you with the Spirit, so that you can have real power to serve Him. Purify your heart, be obedient, and come boldly into His presence with praise. Then let Him fill you.

Don't flee in fear from the moving of the Spirit, when the power of God begins to take hold of your body.

When praying for the Holy Spirit, you will feel a mighty moving of the Spirit upon you. It may cause you to shake (Jer. 23:9), or to tremble (Acts 9:6) or if God's power is mightily present, even to fall (Acts 9:4). Note that when Daniel prayed and sought God, he said, "I fell upon my face." "I was in a deep sleep." Dan. 8:17, 18). Your lips may stammer (Isa. 28:11 with I Cor. 14:21). The Holy Spirit's coming may be accompanied by a vision (see Acts 2:17).

You may even stagger as one drunk (Acts 2:13-15). DO NOT BE AFRAID OF THESE MANIFESTATIONS. Remember that they are scriptural and God-ordained. Others have had one or more of these manifestations when they came into the presence of God, and you may have them too!

BE OBEDIENT. Remember, the Holy Spirit is given to them that are obedient. "So is also the Holy Ghost whom God HATH GIVEN to them that OBEY HIM." Acts 5:32. Yield so completely to the Spirit's power that nothing else matters but doing what God says, whether great or small. Be willing to follow God all the way no matter where or how He may lead.

Pride will keep you from being obedient. Get rid of PRIDE. "God resisteth the proud, but giveth grace to the humble." Jas. 4:6. "The Lord knoweth the proud afar off." Psa. 138:6.

DO NOT RESIST. Remember that Satan knows that if you yield to the Spirit, you will be filled. It is

Satan's plan to tempt you to resist the Spirit. He will tell you, "This is not necessary," or "You can receive the Holy Ghost without all this foolishness." Be on your guard. Resist the devil (and he will flee from you), but DO NOT RESIST THE HOLY SPIRIT! People who resist the Holy Ghost are called, "STIFF NECKED." "Ye stiff necked and uncircumcised in heart and ears, ye do always RESIST THE HOLY GHOST: as your fathers did, so do ye." Acts 7:51.

YIELD YOUR PART! This is important. YOU have a part in the baptism of the Spirit. John likened the baptism of the Holy Ghost to water baptism, for he said, "I indeed baptize you with water, but he shall baptize you with the Holy Ghost and with fire." Matt. 3:11. The word "baptize" means "to dip" or to "put under." When being baptized in water, one must submit to the one doing the baptizing. Just so, one must be yielded if he expects to be baptized with the Spirit. The baptism of the Spirit is Christ submerging every part of our being soul, mind, spirit, hands, tongue, lips, voice, and ALL!

Then, yield fully and let Him possess ALL of your being.

Many yield to the Spirit until they are partially under His control. Their lips and tongue quiver under the control of the Spirit. The Holy Ghost is moving upon them, and ready to come in and speak out, but they WILL NOT YIELD their service, or part, in the baptism. They are praising God in their native tongue, but the Spirit is trying to speak in another language. They stubbornly insist upon saying what THEY WANT TO SAY, in the way they want to say it! If they find they cannot continue to praise God in English, they refuse to speak at all! It is the Spirit that gives the utterance, but you must furnish the SOUND, the LIPS, the TONGUE, and the EFFORT to speak out. The Spirit furnishes the dialect. The Spirit possesses you, and He from within speaks back to God above, using your speaking apparatus as a transmitter, as you yield to Him. This is why some speak right out in "tongues" immediately, while others hold back from fully yielding, because of fear or doubts.

DO NOT BE AFRAID OF RECEIVING SOMETHING YOU HAVEN'T ASKED FOR!

"If a son ask bread of any of you that is a father, will he give him a stone? or if he ask a fish, will he for a fish give him a serpent? or if he shall ask an egg, will he offer him a scorpion? If ye then, being evil, know how to give good gifts unto your children; HOW MUCH MORE SHALL your heavenly father GIVE THE HOLY GHOST TO THEM THAT ASK HIM?" Luke 11:11-13. God said He would give THE HOLY GHOST! Then don't be afraid of getting something else. Just believe God. He cannot lie! Then, in Jesus' name, RECEIVE YE THE HOLY GHOST!

Is it necessary, since the day of Pentecost, to "tarry" or "wait" for the Holy Ghost? Before Pentecost, the disciples tarried in the upper room at Jerusalem, waiting for the "Promise of the Father," the Holy

Ghost, which had not yet been given (John 7:39). From the time that the Holy Ghost was given, on the day of Pentecost, we have no record of any one tarrying for the Holy Ghost. They RECEIVED. The Samaritans did not tarry for the Holy Ghost. Peter and John "prayed for them" and laid hands on them and they received the Holy Ghost (Acts 8:15-17). In the tenth chapter of Acts, the Holy Ghost fell on all who heard the word, even as it was being preached. At Ephesus, there was no long waiting, or tarrying, after they came to the knowledge of the truth. As soon as they had obeyed the word, Paul laid his hands upon them, and they were filled IMMEDIATELY with the Holy Ghost.

It isn't even necessary to wait for the laying on of hands, before you can receive the Holy Ghost. At the house of Cornelius, in Caesarea, all who heard the word received the Holy Ghost WHILE PETER WAS yet SPEAKING! It is entirely scriptural to receive the Holy Ghost during the preaching. Start worshipping God as soon as you come into the service. Come quickly into His presence, with a thankful heart and praise on your lips, expecting God to meet your need. Yield to the Spirit when you feel Him coming upon you, and you can receive the Holy Ghost then and there, without long waiting.

We may liken this experience to a man who is given a vessel, and told to go out and hold his vessel up toward heaven until he has it filled with rain water. If the rain has not started when the man goes out with his vessel, it is easy to see that he will have to "WAIT" until it starts raining before he can fill his vessel. However, if the rain is already pouring down, all he will have to do is to go out where the rain is falling, keep his vessel right side up, and STAY THERE WHILE IT GETS FULL!

In Zechariah, the outpouring of the Spirit is likened to the natural rain that falls from the sky. "Ask ye of the Lord rain in the time of the latter rain." Zech. 10:1. (See also James 5:7). The rain began to fall on the day of Pentecost. It is falling today. All you need to do now is to get where the (spiritual) rain is falling, and get your vessel full! WAITING IS NOT NECESSARY! WHY NOT BE FILLED NOW? THIS VERY MOMENT!

I do not want the reader to think that I am discouraging prayer. I am not. Few today pray as much as they should. There is a "waiting" upon God that is profitable and I certainly encourage it. Isaiah said, "They that 'wait' upon the Lord shall renew their strength; mount up as with wings." Isa. 40:31. Daniel prayed or "waited" upon God for three whole weeks. Christ Himself "continued all night in prayer." Certainly God's people everywhere today need to get back on their knees and wait upon GOD IN BELIEVING PRAYER! The waiting upon GOD IN PRAYER will condition one's heart for the Holy Ghost. However, after one is ready to receive this experience, the promise must then be claimed. What waiting or tarrying we should do today should only be to condition our hearts in preparation FOR the Holy Spirit. In other words, let us "wait" or tarry only as long as is necessary to get our vessel or "temple" cleansed for the Spirit's abiding place. Remember He will come to dwell only in CLEAN temples.

Waiting or tarrying in itself, alone, will never fill one with the Holy Ghost. If that were enough then why have some people 'tarried' or "waited' for thirty five years and are still waiting and have received nothing! Furthermore, they may NEVER receive unless they do MORE than wait. If 'tarrying' alone was enough to receive this experience, then EVERYONE today that tarried (waited) WOULD BE FILLED! Thousands today declare that they have been 'tarrying' for many years and with 'all' their tarrying they as yet have not received! This is evidence that one must DO MORE than tarry. One must consecrate, obey, yield, believe and RECEIVE! Why not NOW?

CHAPTER 6

THE LAYING ON OF HANDS TO RECEIVE THE HOLY GHOST

It is as scriptural to lay hands upon those seeking the Holy Ghost as it is to lay hands upon those who are in need of healing. Believers are commanded to lay hands upon the sick (Mark 16:18). Note that, "By the hands of the apostles were many signs and wonders wrought among the people." Acts 5:12.

The laying on of hands is a fundamental doctrine, as is water baptism. Heb. 6:2.

Following, I quote from other Assemblies of God authors on this all-important subject of the laying on of hands to receive the Holy Ghost.

Ralph M. Riggs *The Spirit Himself*

Gospel Pub. House, 1949.

"Samaritans Believed And Were Prayed For." The apostles laid hands on them (as an aid to the seeker's faith) and they received the Holy Spirit (through laying on of hands) Acts 8:17. God honored His servants by imparting the Holy Spirit through the laying on of their hands that the people might honor them as God-appointed and God-honored leaders (Pg.109).

"Paul Prayed And Was Prayed For. He may not have known what he needed, but God knew, and sent Ananias that he might receive his sight and be filled with the Holy Ghost.

Ananias put his hands on him as he prayed for him. This is a method which is common in Divine prac-tice. This symbol that the one who is praying is a channel through whom the power of the Lord is con-veyed for healing or for blessing." (Pg.110)

"Ephesians Believed And Were Prayed For. At Ephesus, Paul care-fully instructed those disciples of

John, laid hands on them and they, too, received the Holy Spirit. Who would say that he did not instruct them according to the pattern which had been followed theretofore? It is the once-for-all pattern: be saved, obey God, ask Him for His blessings, believe with all your heart, and ye shall receive the fullness of the Holy Spirit." (Pgs. 111, 112)

Myer Pearlman *Knowing The Doctrines Of The Bible*, Gospel Pub. House, 1937:

"Weinel, a German theologian, says inspirational sessions were held till well on into the second century. The Holy Ghost, he states, was communicated to converts by the laying on of hands and prayer and wrought signs and wonders. Inspirational sessions would seem to describe special services for those who desired to receive the Spirit's power." (Pg. 317)

With Signs Following, Gospel Pub. House, 1946. Listed: 1951 Cat. Number 2B 636, Page 135 (First Edition 1926, Second Edition 1928).

"Augustine in the fourth century: 'We still do what the apostles did when they laid hands on the Samaritans and called down the Holy Spirit on them by laying on of hands. It is expected the converts speak with new tongues.' " (Pg. 254)

J. Roswell Flower, General Secretary, Assemblies of God, The Pentecostal Evangel, Official Organ of the Assemblies of God November 26, 1950. *Birth of the Pentecostal Movement.*

"The first step having been taken, it was logical that hunger should develop among the students for an experience which would measure up to the pattern found in the second chapter of the Acts of the Apostles. We will now permit Miss Agnes N. Ozman to tell her own story, as recorded in WITH SIGNS FOLLOWING:'"

"In the fall of 1900 a Bible school was opened at Topeka, Kansas. We will let one of the students, Mrs. Agnes N. O. LaBerge, formerly Miss Agnes N. Ozman, who was the first to receive the Baptism in the Holy

Ghost in the school, tell her story:'
"It was nearly eleven o'clock on this
first of January (1901) that it came
into my heart to ask that hands be
laid upon me that I might receive
the gift of the Holy Ghost. As hands
were laid upon my head the Holy
Spirit fell upon me, and I began to
speak in tongues, glorifying God. I
talked several languages. It was as
though rivers of living water were
proceeding from my innermost being." (Pgs. 19, 20)

(Brother Flower, then, described
the experience of another student,
adding a footnote of his own expla-
nation of certain phases of their experiences:)

"Another student, Miss Lillian
Thistlewaite, who also received a
similar experience, wrote of the
Spirit being manifested in the
school at that time, as follows:

'"The presence of the Lord was
very real and there were definite
heart-searchings. I was not looking
for tongues but for some evidence
from God that would convince me
that I had received the Baptism. We

prayed for ourselves and we prayed for one another. I never felt so little and so utterly nothing before.' Then through the Spirit I received this message in my soul; 'Praise the Lord for the Baptism, for the Spirit does come in by faith through the laying on of hands[1]. 'I tried to praise Him in English but could not, so I just let the praise come as it would in this new language that was given."

Maynard L. Ketcham, Field Secretary for India, Assemblies of God *Pentecost In The Ganges Delta*

"But what of Brother Abdul Munshie, the important figure, the one for whose special benefit prayer was being made? Seeing the desperation of our brother, wife and I were led to lay our bands on him and claim definitely the desired fullness. And without delay, the Holy Spirit did come in and take control, and manifest His presence in unspeakable glory. To our Brother Munshie was given a beautiful new tongue, and for hours English and his native Bengali were forgotten." (Pgs. 12, 13)

Donald Gee *Upon All Flesh* Gospel Pub. House, 1947.

W. F. P. Burton'Belgian Congo "Not many minutes after we started praying the first few were filled with the Spirit; and then they helped us by laying hands upon, and praying with the others." (Pgs. 71, 72)

Smith Wigglesworth *Faith That Prevails* Gospel Pub. House 1938.

The account of how he received the Baptism: "I went to the Vicarage that day to say good-bye and I said to Sister Goddy, the vicar's wife, 'I am going away, but I have not received the tongues yet.' She said, 'It isn't tongues you need, but the Baptism.' I said, 'I have the Baptism, Sister, but I would like to have you lay hands on me before I leave.' She laid her hands on me and then had to go out of the room. The fire fell. ... As I was extolling, magnifying, and praising Him I was speaking in tongues as the Spirit of God gave me utterance. I knew now that I had received the real Baptism in the Holy Ghost." (Pgs. 33, 34)

Ever Increasing Faith, Pg. 100; Smith Wigglesworth, Apostle of Faith, Gospel Publishing House. 1948, Pgs . 45, 46).

"I (Wigglesworth) laid my hands on his head and said, 'Receive ye the Holy Ghost!' Instantly the power of God fell upon him and he began breathing very heavily. He rolled off the chair and there he lay like a bag of potatoes, utterly helpless. . . . Then to our joy he began speaking in tongues." (Pgs. 43, 44)

Smith Wigglesworth *Ever Increasing Faith* Gospel Publishing House, 1924.

"I went up and down laying hands upon people that they might receive the Holy Ghost, and they were speaking in tongues.'" (Pg. 152)

Evangelist Gayle Jackson *Pentecostal Evangel* November 12, 1950. A message at the annual convention of the Pentecostal Fellowship of North America. Pg. 3.

"God said, 'You will lay your hands upon them and they will receive the Holy Ghost instantly.' I told the audience in Biloxi what God had told me He was going to do. We moved from Biloxi to the next meeting. One night the mighty power of God fell, and 1,500 men and women came rushing to the front to be filled with the Spirit of God. The mighty receiving meeting was on, and that night 500 men and women were baptized in the Holy Ghost. Every one of them spoke in tongues and glorified God." (Pg. 4)

I do not believe nor teach, nor do I practice the bestowing or confirming of "Spiritual

Gifts" by the laying on of hands. It has been my happy privilege in many recent campaigns to see many receive and exercise the "Gifts" without imposition of hands. I do, however, believe the Bible teaches there is a profitable laying on of hands for the receiving of the Holy Ghost. It is well to remember that there also can be an unprofitable and unscriptural laying on of hands. I Tim. 5:22.

True, one can be filled with the Holy Ghost without hands being layed upon him, as in Acts 2 or Acts

10. Many also receive healing without anyone laying on their hands. Although this is possible, one must remember it is ALSO SCRIPTURAL to lay hands upon those who are in need of the Holy Ghost.

Samaria had a great revival with many saved, blessed and healed. However, none of the converts had received the Holy Ghost under Philip's ministry. It would seem in the light of this scripture, that although Philip was a man mightily anointed of God, he did not enjoy the ministry of laying on of hands. It was no doubt for this reason, "When the apostles which were at Jerusalem, heard that Samaria had received the word of God, they SENT (it must have been important) unto them Peter and John; who prayed for them then layed their hands upon them and they received the Holy Ghost." Acts 8:14-17.

The apostle Paul (Acts 19) must have had the ministry of laying on of hands also. He found certain disciples at Ephesus who had not received the Holy Ghost but, "When

Paul had layed his hands upon them, the Holy Ghost came upon them'." Acts 19:6.

Something mighty occurs when, in the name of the Lord (as His agents, under divine commission, doing His work in His absence), MEN OF FAITH lay hands upon those who IN FULL FAITH RECEIVE THE IMPARTATION. The impartation must be RECEIVED as well as IMPARTED in FULL FAITH!

The laying on of hands does not heal the sick nor fill the believer. It is God who heals and fills the believer through faith. Obedience to the ordinance of laying on of hands quickens one's faith, giving God His full opportunity of imparting heavenly blessing. God by sovereign grace, promises His power through the ordinance when it is performed in obedience and received through vital faith.

It has been the happy privilege of the author to see literally hundreds of people in a single service receive this mighty infilling as hands were laid upon believers who were ready and have come believing.

If you are in a service where hands are being laid upon believers for the infilling of the Spirit, be sure that before hands are laid upon you, you are prayed through to a place of real victory and faith, so that you can in faith receive the impartation. Immediately when hands are laid upon you, YIELD YOUR PART, BE-LIEVE AND RECEIVE THE HOLY SPIRIT!

After you have been filled, STAY FULL of the Spirit! There is but one filling, but there are many refill-ings. Get refilled in every service you attend. KEEP YOUR LAMPS FILLED AND BURNING BRIGHT! "Be not drunken with wine but be filled with the spirit." Eph. 5:18. Literally, STAY FULL OF THE HOLY

[1] Bro. Flower: "The practice of the lay-ing on of hands for the receiving of the Holy Spirit is Scriptural (Acts 8:17, 18; 9:17; 19:6), but is not the only means by which the Holy Spirit may be received (Acts 2:1-4; 10:44, 45; 11; 15), as many

thousands of baptized believers can testify. Even though there may be the laying on of hands, a definite scriptural Baptism in the Holy Spirit is made possible by a number of elements. The primary factor is FAITH (Gal. 2:2, 4, 14; John 7:38). Another factor is spiritual hunger or thirst (John 7:37; Matt. 5:6). Obedience is also mentioned in the Scriptures (Acts 5:32). If the proper groundwork has been laid, which includes heart cleansing, spiritual hunger, full obedience to the will of God, and faith in the promises of God'laying on of hands may become the focal point for one's faith as evidenced in the testimonies recorded herewith." (Pgs. 3, 12)

CHAPTER 7

ARE THE PENTECOSTAL MANIFESTATIONS SCRIPTURAL?

Through the entire Bible, God has admonished His people to "Praise ye the Lord";

"Shout unto God"; "Clap your hands"; "Praise God in His sanctuary"; "Rejoice evermore"; "Praise Him in the dance"; "Make a joyful noise unto the Lord." Furthermore it has been encouraged as a part of Scriptural worship! This chapter is not offered as a complete treatise on this subject but is just a few thoughts in outline form to show that the manifestations seen and heard in Pentecostal services are scriptural, and the plan of God for His people in worship.

In this chapter, many scriptures from the Old Testament are used. Although some reading this may believe that no Old Testament references should be used today, I call to your attention that Christ Himself divided the Old Testament into three sections, the law of Moses, the prophets, and the psalms. Luke 24:44. The only portion of the Old Testament that has been "done away" with was the law observances which have been nailed to the cross. Col. 2:14. This leaves the prophets and the psalms from which I feel free to quote freely.

PRAISE

God's people, whether Old or New Testament saints, are called to "show forth the praises of him who hath called you out of darkness." I Pet. 2:9-10. We are told to "Offer up a sacrifice of praise to God CONTINUALLY." Heb. 13:15. David says, "At ALL times." Psm. 34:1. We are told that the "Dead praise NOT the Lord," Psm. 115:17; but that "Praise is comely for the upright," Psm. 33:1. It is scriptural to praise God "In the house of the Lord." Psm. 135:2. "In the congregation." Psm. 22:25. "In his sanctuary," Psm. 150:1-6. In fact, we are taught to, "Enter into his gates with thanksgiving and into his court with praise." Psm. 100:4, Psm. 42:4. Note the results of PRAISE in both Old and New Testament, 2 Chron. 5:13-14 and Luke 24:53 with Acts 2:1-4. Why shouldn't Satan discourage praise in the worship service today? He knows what happened in the past when people included PRAISE in their worship services. HE IS AFRAID it will happen again if people get away from their forms! Note that when skeptics disapproved praise, CHRIST STAMPED HIS APPROVAL UPON IT! Luke 19:37-40.

God begs for it today, "Oh, that men would praise the Lord'." Psm. 107:8.

Will you by your silent indifference, cause God to continue to BEG YOU to praise Him?

"LET EVERYTHING THAT HATH BREATH, PRAISE THE LORD!"

Psm. 150:6.

NOISE

"O come, let us sing unto the Lord: let us make a JOYFUL NOISE to the rock of our salvation. Let us come before his presence (go to church) with thanksgiving and make a joyful NOISE'." Psm. 95:1. See also, Psm. 100:1; Psm. 81:1. Some may say they do not believe in making noise in church. In other words, they disagree with God and what His word teaches. They don't believe in doing what GOD WANTS THEM TO DO!

Evidently they are out of harmony with God. Why not worship God the way HE wants you to instead of the way man ("form that denies the power thereof") wants? As long as the "noise" is joyful, certainly it is scriptural! God wants His people to serve Him with GLADNESS! "Serve the Lord with GLADNESS." Psm. 100:2. "Let the saints be JOYFUL." Psm. 149:5. We are told to, "Make his praise GLORIOUS!" Psm. 66:1. Even when we are playing instruments unto the Lord we are exhorted to, "Play skillfully with a

LOUD noise." Psm. 33:2. Note what happens to the enemy when God's people shout. They said, " Woe unto us." I Sam. 4:7. When God's people worship God again as He desires, it will again be "WOE" to the enemy!

CLAPPING OF HANDS

"0 clap your hands all ye people; shout unto God with the voice of triumph." Psm. 47:1. Some may say, "Why should I do that?" If for no other reason than because God tells you to, THAT SHOULD BE ENOUGH! Another will say, "I don't feel like doing that." I have found that when the REAL JOY and GLADNESS of salvation comes, people are going to feel like doing what God tells them they ought to be doing! See also Psm. 98:4-9; Isa. 55:12.

HANDS UPRAISED

"Lift up your HANDS IN THE SANCTUARY, and bless the Lord." (Psm. 134:2) "Thus will I bless thee while I live: I will lift up my hands in thy name." (Psm. 63:4) God blesses us by giving unto us all good things.

We can in return (if we aren't too stubborn) bless the Lord by praising Him with upraised hands. See also 1 Tim. 2:8 which reads, "I will therefore that men pray everywhere LIFTING UP HOLY HANDS!"

DANCE

Solomon declared there was a time for all things, including "A TIME TO DANCE." Eccl. 3:4. David danced before the Lord "WITH ALL HIS MIGHT." 2 Sam. 6:14. He further states that we are to "Praise his name in the DANCE." (Psm. 149:3) (See also Jer. 31:13) When Miriam was delivered from captivity and bondage she danced! (Exo. 15:20) So did "all the women" (see same verse). It could be that many today are more in bondage than they realize. In bondage to pride, fear (of persecution), coldness, indifference or perhaps unyieldedness.

LEAPING

See Luke 6:23; Acts 3:8; Acts 14:10; 2 Sam. 6:16; Psm. 18:29; Luke 1:41.

LAUGHTER

Psm. 126:2; Gen. 21:6; Eccl. 3:4; Luke 6:21; Job 8:21.

WEEPING

Psm. 51:17; Psm. 42:3; Psm. 126:5; Isa. 16:9; Lam. 2:18; 2 Cor. 2:4; Acts 20:19. PRAYING TOGETHER Acts 4:23-24; 1 Tim. 2:8; Mk. 11:17.

SHAKING

The apostle Paul met the Lord on the road to Damascus. He not only "fell" to the earth but also heard a voice. He was in the mighty presence of the Lord! In that mighty presence, Paul "TREMBLED!" Acts 9:6. Under the same conditions, Daniel declared, "I stood trembling." Daniel 10:11. Jeremiah said, "All my bones shake because of the LORD." Jer. 23:9. See also Hab. 3:16; Job 16:12. The author will challenge anyone to come into the mighty presence of the Lord without having some kind of a supernatural manifestation.

FALLING PROSTRATE

Because of God's presence, Paul

NOT ONLY TREMBLED, BUT "FELL TO THE EARTH." Acts 9:4. Jeremiah, "because of the Lord," not only shook BUT WAS LIKE A MAN OVERCOME WITH WINE! Jer. 23:9. Daniel said, "When he came where I stood, I FELL UPON MY FACE." Dan. 8:17. John said, "When I saw him, I FELL AT HIS FEET AS DEAD." Rev. 1:17. Here, one may ask, "but can we come into the presence of the Lord like that today?" Why not? Only iniquity can separate us from God.

Isaiah 59:2. One can still come into God's presence as of old if he seeks God. Furthermore when one does come into the holy presence of AL-MIGHTY GOD, certainly it is scriptural today to act as people did yesterday! Jesus said, "Where two or three are gathered together (in church) in my name, THERE AM I IN THE MIDST OF THEM." Matt. 18:20. Worship becomes VERY REAL when this truth is realized! It will no longer be a form!

QUIVERING LIPS

Hab. 3:16; Isa. 28:9-13 with 1 Cor. 14:21.

TRANCE

Ac. 22:17; Ac . 10:10; Ac. 2:17.

SPEAKING IN TONGUES

Read chapter four of this book. Read the twelfth chapter of 1 Corinthians. THEN GIVE GOD THE PRIVILEGE OF MAKING HIMSELF REAL TO YOU!

Printed by BoD™in Norderstedt, Germany